Bishop Eddie L. Long

The Untold Story

The Story of Adversity, Pain, and Resilience

Printed in the United States of America

Book Design & Branding:
PDG Branding & Marketing
www.pdgbranding.com

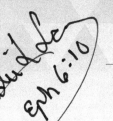

The UNTOLD STORY
EDDIE L LONG

Table of Contents

Special Thanks:

First, I have to thank God for allowing me the opportunity to share all of these thoughts with you! I want to personally thank my loving wife, Dr. Vanessa Long; all of my children and grandchildren whom I love so much; and the entire New Birth Church family that is steadily growing. I would also like to thank The Father's House Pastors for always standing with me, and all of my true friends and loved ones that have supported me throughout the years.

— Bishop Eddie Long

INTRODUCTION

I see this book as much more than just a collection of words. These words became sentences; these sentences became paragraphs; these paragraphs became chapters; these chapters evolved in to conversations; and these conversations have been used to shape and impact my life; in which serve as a gateway of possibility for you to see a world of truths and life. As a minister of the gospel for the majority of my life, I have learned many invaluable life principles through lessons. The goal of this book is to impart the wisdom I've gained into your life and to share my overall vision for how to strengthen the church in our tumultuous times.

I have come to peace with much of what has occurred in my life over the last few years. Though incredibly painful, there were many principles that were necessary for me to learn. Subsequently, with great deliberation and difficulty, I have resolved within myself that what is most important is to focus on acceptance

acceptance

and discover true happiness. Happiness is the power of acceptance, and the ability to accept what is and what is not. These crucial principles are imparted and shared for the purpose of a global impact by which we can discover our own humanity. I believe this allows us understanding in that which makes us human.

Beyond developing a more crystallized sense of God's purpose for my life, I have come to realize that there are underlying themes that have divinely guided me. In being reminded of this underlying current, I feel a greater sense of focus and empowerment in focusing on the future and what I have been called to do. That is only possible because I am committed to a future that is bigger than myself. I have lived from this perspective for many years; however it means more to mean now than previously.

Failing is not my greatest fear. Rather, my greatest fear is of succeeding at doing the wrong thing. Which I will call my identity... My greatest fear is being a casualty of my own success.

The UNTOLD STORY

EDDIE L. LONG

Never could I have imagined that my greatest victories would become open doors to my greatest challenges. Suddenly, almost overnight it seemed, everything I had accomplished became a platform for searing criticism. If I were going to survive the storm, I had to learn to shift my perspective of my present circumstances from doom and gloom to optimism and purpose. The key to true spiritual strength lies there, in the development of perspective. In the coming pages, I will detail not only how perspective saved my life but I will also outline how it can ultimately save yours.

Chapter One
WHAT I LEARNED ABOUT MYSELF

1 Corinthians 10:12

*"Therefore let him who thinks he stands
take heed lest he fall."*

EDDIE L LONG

The UNTOLD STORY

EDDIE L. LONG

Every individual is shaped by life experiences. While this is not a groundbreaking thought, most of us never consider it until we face trials and tests. Throughout my adult life and ministry, I always assumed that I fully knew myself, until I faced the most challenging season in my life, the season of my identity. I learned the hard way that I had become addicted to trying to be everything to everyone.

Years of tireless work, sacrifice—and, more importantly, God's blessings—had opened doors that I never could have imagined. Requests for the church to offer philanthropic help was coming from all directions and angles, and I tried to fulfill them all. Through the success of our church, I was given opportunities very few ministers ever have: to be the keynote speaker in the presence of thousands; to be respected and acknowledged by everyone in the room; to be watched and stopped by people who wanted to talk with me. There were literally days that I would come to my office and find myself overwhelmed by the stack of invitations to speak at churches and events all over the country and various parts of the world. At first, the travel and amenities were humbling. After a while, however, it became addicting and I fell into the "Christian celebrity" trap. It is this trap that began to shape my way of being and causing concern as I look at this generation of Christians.

Our current church culture can unintentionally feed a celebrity mindset. If a minister isn't careful, he or she can quickly be drawn into it. *The celebrity mindset is created by overexposure to people, but underexposure to God, and it occurs subtly.*

I was speaking somewhere every weekend not to mention my responsibilities to New Birth and new invitations just kept pouring in. In my ministry-driven mind, I told myself that I was preaching the Gospel and helping people. I realized that if you aren't careful, you can become more preoccupied with creating the need to be seen. It is tempting and far too easy to become a Christian celebrity who lives by following the rules of what became my identity trap.

REMEMBER what (God) (alled you FoR!,

MY IDENTITY TRAP

• ID TRAP I: Celebrities love other celebrities. *The art of "name dropping" reaches a different stratosphere when you enter the celebrity realm. Who you meet, who you know, and who you speak with is even more important than it was before. It creates an inflated sense of self-worth and purpose. Slowly, the emphasis is no longer on Jesus but on you.*

Keep God 1st.

• ID TRAP II: Celebrities like being seen with other celebrities. *Selfies become "events" when you are a celebrity. People point you out. People want to be seen with you. I can't tell you how many times someone has asked if they could take a picture with me. It all starts as a benign event, but after a while, you want to be noticed. It feeds the celebrity ego. You actually begin to desire the ultimate selfie which is when you are seen with other celebrities.*

• ID TRAP III: Celebrities love talking about other celebrities. *If you are a celebrity, then you know the real story of what's happening in other people's lives. You bring it up innocently; or without asking, people willingly volunteer information. I came to this realization one day when a friend said to me:*

> "You have become a conduit to the ultimate inside information. You have reached the inner circle. Everyone talks to you."

• ID TRAP IV: Celebrities turn against other celebrities more often than not. *The speed with which celebrities will turn against each other is amazing. Some allow their love of position and image to often exceed their love for people. In the blink of an eye, you might be told, "I can't be seen with you or else it may affect my status."*

This addiction unknowingly opened the door for a major, sudden downfall. I went from being the person everyone wanted on the platform to the person that no one would be seen with. I was being forced to learn one of the most important leadership principles I've ever heard: "God will never allow your love for the stage to exceed your love for Him. Anytime the pastor's name precedes the church, it is a sign of impending trouble."

It was a trap that I had fallen into. I began to pay more attention to the rules of being a celebrity than the rules of God. I needed to be reminded that Jesus doesn't take second billing to anyone. He must always be first.

This is easier said than done, especially once you have received a high level of recognition that can appear impossible to let go. It's such a powerful feeling that can be difficult to redirect.

We see on the news, time and time again, how many celebrities crash and burn. When you live in the spotlight, it's easy to develop a false sense of identity that is based on how others define you rather than who you really are. When this happens, you ultimately become someone else.

Humility, however, is God's providential tool for bringing a person back to reality. In the Scriptures, John the Baptist cautions that when we are increasing, there is a chance that God is decreasing. We must decrease so that He may increase in us and in the sight of others. In His wisdom, God humbled me so that I would wake up and re-commit myself to fulfilling His life purposes and not Eddie Long's life purposes! God wanted me to re-examine my heart and my motives for doing what I was called to do.

Fortunately, I was able to find my way out of the maze by heeding the wake-up call. I admitted to myself, but more importantly, to God that my life had become too hectic and fast-paced. I took responsibility for allowing my life to become so busy that I was distracted from the true assignment God had given to me.

Looking back on it, one of the greatest things I learned about myself is that I defined myself as a person who wants to and believes that he can solve any problem. This is the one thing that anyone who is close to me knows— I have a Superman complex.

My favorite superhero has always been Superman. It stems from something that was embedded deep into my psyche as a child. Even to this day, I have a statue of Superman on my desk, and my office is filled with

Superman-related memorabilia gifts from friends.

There is something about the idea of being a
protector and a rescuer that has stuck with me. Over time,
it became fully intertwined with my life calling. In fact, my
motivation was never to be famous. I was purely motivated
to be in as many places as possible to help as many people
as possible.

Believe it or not, I never charged an honorarium
or fee when deciding to accept an invitation to speak. My
addiction was not to money but solely to helping everyone
I could possibly help. There was good in my drive to be a
blessing to others but my inability to maintain a healthy
balance of when to give was my undoing. I have learned
when one's identity is broken down based on the traps I
mentioned previously, it can be incapable to function with
integrity.

The addiction to helping became so strong that I felt
a sense of obligation. I felt I had to go and couldn't ever say
"No." Over time, I gradually stopped listening to my body
and the warning signs. All along, it was telling me I was

exhausted and needed to slow down. I ignored the feeling that my schedule was out of control while I raced from one airport to another. Simply put I was no longer running my life; the identity traps were running me.

So many things were coming at me and the church was exploding. I thought everything was grand, but to be honest, my crash was inevitable. On the surface, I was a success at doing everything, but I couldn't keep track of fulfilling my true life purpose.

I was doing things that didn't ultimately matter and weren't relevant to growing the Kingdom of God. I may have told myself that they were, but it wasn't true. I was just keeping myself busy. I said "Yes" to a BET exercise and fitness show. It sounded good at the time for the sake of exposure and visibility, but clearly that's not why God put me in my position.

My focus had to come back. My priorities were so out of balance that when my friends had a death in their family, I was too busy to go support them at the funeral. I couldn't stop myself and say "No." If a call came in, I was out the door once again trying to be Superman. As a result, many important relationships suffered greatly.

When your identity defines you like many of us have been guilty of allowing it to do everyday you will be living with a distorted definition of success, happiness and fulfillment. More than anything, I lost sight of God's big picture for my life and for those with whom I was entrusted with the ability to directly influence. I forgot that Jesus was only moved by purpose and never just by need.

A great illustration of this can be found in John 5 when Jesus went to the pool of Bethsaida. While there were many people in the crowd who needed healing, Jesus went to just one man and asked him if he wanted to be healed.

If that were me, without hesitation or a second thought, I would have gone to each and every sick person. On top of that, I would have had a crusade and marched across the stage—all in an attempt to help everyone at the pool.

My life today is night and day in comparison to where I was spiritually. My perspective and approach to life is totally different. I've regained my focus combined with a greater sense of balance regarding who to serve, when to serve, and how to serve, instead of selling myself out.

One of my best teachers in this area has been my wife. I used her words of wisdom as a barometer for gauging how much of myself I am supposed to directly give to any area of serving others. She would constantly tell me, "You have a big vision. Your vision is so big that it's a three lifetime or three-generation vision. This means that you have to discern how much of the work should be done by you and how much should be accomplished by the future generations."

These words were profound and vital to my growth. My wife's words were so powerful that they sparked an 'aha' moment for me; they have helped me greatly in determining when and how much to give. Even more, adding this to my newfound understanding of the wisdom of Jesus who was only moved by purpose and never by need, they also inspired a whole new slogan for the church. Rather than "Bishop Long and New Birth," our new ministry slogan became "We Are New Birth." I went from an "I" to a "WE"; that in itself is an amazing part of the untold story.

The ministry and work of New Birth needed to shine brighter than the name of Eddie Long. In order for this to happen, I had to shift my entire approach to ministry. Before, I was trying to do the work of the ministry rather than equipping the people to do the work of the ministry. Now, I am trusting other members of the church with greater levels of responsibility.

Just recently, I sent a delegation to Charleston, South Carolina, to assist the believers there in their time of tragedy, where in times past I would have felt the need to be there. I now understand that the work of the ministry is still being done even when I am not physically present. The reach of what we are doing can now be far greater. Now the power is seen and manifested as a body and not as a singular unit. St. Paul echoes those sentiments when he shares, "It is no longer I but Christ."

The reality is that no one is the energizer bunny and no one person keeps anything running. It takes an entire team for the broad scope of God's higher purposes and vision to be fulfilled. I had to embrace humility with the reminder that "Even without Eddie Long, life will go on." I had to be reminded not to think too highly of myself. I had to think from the body of Christ rather than thinking from Eddie's mind.

Just as Daniel needed something to threaten his life to move him into another dimension, I can hear God's voice and message for my life more clearly and with greater intensity. The confirmation I received from God is that there is still much work for me to do. The promise that God has given me is that I am to be a prophet to many nations. The major question in my life now is, "Do I have enough time to accomplish all that God has for me to do while I'm on this earth?" At age 62, I feel as though I'm working much smarter than I did ten or twenty years ago.

The way that I will fulfill God's vision and purpose for my life will be totally different. It will be done with balance and greater humility. I am now more content with living in the moment and taking life one day at a time. Having succumbed to the identity trap, celebrity mindset, I understand the importance of being in a perpetual state of prayer with constant recalibration of my heart and my motives. This is to ensure that I remain humble and focused on what God has called me to do rather than being distracted by what others may want me to do. I refuse to let others drive the conversation of my reformed identity in Christ.

Chapter Two

WHAT I LEARNED
ABOUT FRIENDS

EDDIE L LONG

I t doesn't matter what level of status an individual has attained; friendship is a quality that will always have tremendous value. A rich man, just as a poor man, needs to know what individuals he can trust. A rich man, just as a poor man, loses much and still experiences great pain when he feels betrayed.

Friendship, however, is a quality that is often neglected. For many, it's not until the storms of life come raging that one discovers the need for a solid support system. The question, then, is when you are faced with adversity, will you grow or regress? Will you be swallowed up by hurt and disappointment or embrace a new sense of love and forgiveness? It usually takes a friend to bring the identity to the cross. Judas brought Christ's identity to the crucifixion. All things work together for our good. Because life is about growth and development. Look for where there is an attack it reveals a space for growth and development.

I resolved to become a better friend, a more forgiving person, and a more loving ally. At the same time, I gained even greater clarity as to what it means to be a true companion and why they are so valuable. As friends are an extension of family, they're meant to be there through tough times.

Unfortunately, as a minister I thought I could be a friend to everyone. In the midst of focusing so much of my time and energy on giving to others, I didn't pay close attention to the motives of those around me. I was reckless in how I invested my time into relationships that ultimately amounted to very little value. Therefore, it became a learning curve and a space for me to personally grow and develop.

Many of us are guilty of the same mistake as we allow people into our inner circle who don't have the ability to fully appreciate what we have to share. This brings to mind the biblical verse: "Do not throw your pearls before swine."[1] I am also comforted by the poignant quote from my friend Bishop Will Thornton: "*If you can't get with my cargo, you can't get on my ship.* "

The lessons I have since learned from these words of wisdom and other life experiences, is that you should never

---

1 Matthew 7:6

honor someone with the title of friend until they've earned
it. Relationships need to go through certain stages before
they are solidified. You never know who your friends
are until you go through tough times and face adversity.
In these times, friendships truly are tested and ulterior
motives are exposed.

      Discerning the motives of other individuals can be a
very difficult lesson to master. This is why I want to stress
the importance of taking ownership for how one evaluates
friendships. Know and accept that all relationships must
go through a minimum of three stages: the "honeymoon";
the "settling in" stage; and, the "conflict" stage. The
'honeymoon" stage is the beginning stage of a relationship.
You have just met and share common interests while
bonding and growing together. In the "settling in" stage,
people get comfortable with one another and develop
routines. Then, at some point—whether its six months
or two years later—there is the "conflict stage." This is
a time where a major crisis is experienced in one of the
individual's lives or directly between the two.

Conflict and tension can arise from anywhere. You might be going through a divorce and your friend might not be as supportive as you would expect. Your friend might lose his job and asks to borrow money but your answer is "No." Whatever source precipitates the conflict, your relationship at some point "will be tested." It is in the testing that you discover who your true friends are.

Another great illustration of relationship growth is the "seven stages of friendship." I believe that most people can easily relate to these:

> ➤ **Stage 1 - "I Think You're Cool":** Whether it be the initial encounter or the first few casual meetings, people tend to gravitate toward each other when they have a familiarity. You start to notice the same person or group of people; and, in your mind, they become "cool."

> ➤ **Stage 2 - "Does (He/She) Return My Feelings":** The foundation of communication starts to form at this stage. You are now at a point of conversation and exchanging ideas. You also begin to wonder what the other person

thinks and if their thoughts are in line with your feelings. The sharing of thoughts leads to different viewpoints, and you gain insight on the other person's thinking.

> **Stage 3 - "Let's Hang Out":** This stage changes everything as you are now outside of your original comfort zone. Maybe you grab something to eat or attend a social event that you both are interested in. This requires an exchange of contact information for planning. If executed right, you start to create memories with your new friend.

> **Stage 4 - "You Should Meet My Posse":** After a successful one-on-one encounter, you begin to consider this person a friend; however, you need more opinions. You like the way they conduct themselves, and you are already confident that they would blend well with your crew of friends. A familiar friend's gathering or a regular meet-up is a great way to introduce this new potential friend to your proven friends.

➢ **Stage 5 - "OK, We're officially Friends" :** The meet-up went well and everyone else likes this new person you are hanging out with. So, now you're friends. You communicate by phone, text, email, you become friends on social media. At this point, you have met significant others, maybe parents and have possibly hung out. You have traded secrets, and shared history, along with funny stories. You are officially friends.

➢ **Stage 6 - "Can We Survive This Separation":** Friendships, like all relationships, go through trials. One major obstacle to maintain a friendship is the separation of the two friends. This separation can be caused by a host of reasons. Unintentional separation can be caused by someone unexpectedly having to relocate because of work, family emergency and educational opportunities. Intentional separation can arise from disagreements and conflict. This stage is when the friendship is truly tested.

> **Stage 7 - "We Made It":** If connection lasts through the rough times and times of separation, the friendship is truly solidified at this stage. Connection is exciting, and you move forward by sharing more experiences and making more memories. By making it through all these stages, you have a true friend who will support you forever. [2]

The overall point I'm trying to make is that the dynamics of relationships are a never-ending and essential part of life. Learning how to evaluate friendships doesn't just apply to me; it's something that we're all faced with. It's up to each of us individually to develop the highest level of discernment for who will remain in our circle. We each have to take responsibility for the warning signs that will inevitably appear when an individual proves to be unworthy of our friendship.

Even Jesus was confronted with the challenge of determining who to honor with the title of "friend." It wasn't until the end—when he was crucified on the cross—that

2 http://hellogiggles.com/stages-friendship-potential-bestie/

he discovered who his true friends really were. Until that point, the 12 disciples were just his associates.

Out of the twelve disciples, only Peter, James and John were trustworthy of reaching a certain level of friendship. Even more, they possessed a range of personality characteristics that created an interesting and necessary dynamic within the group. Peter was a fighter. James was an intellectual. John had a big heart that loved unconditionally and had a very nurturing spirit.

Collectively, one of the most significant attributes they all possessed was that they were *protectors*. The Bible speaks of an incident in which a lady stepped up from out of the crowd, touched Jesus, and was healed. Jesus immediately asked, "Who touched Me?" His perspective on the situation was much different. He saw the heart of the woman and knew that she was authentic. That's why when the lady stepped up to touch Jesus she was instantly healed. There was healing simply in the power of touch. The power of the touch met the internal dialog and created the miracle. Without the dialogue the touch would have brought forth nothing.[3]

3 Luke 8:43-48

The point I want you to take away from this story is not of the protectiveness of the disciples. What resonates with me most about this story is that there were many people around Jesus who touched him physically, but very few touched him spiritually. I see myself in that story as one of many leaders who allow themselves to become surrounded by people who are physically there but spiritually absent.

I got lost in having people around me who didn't really know who I truly was. They didn't fully understand what God had called me to do. I failed to find the right discernment in the range of friends I allowed into my inner circle.

This isn't to say that I didn't have some great friends available to me. I want you to consider who you're interacting with on a daily basis—the people you spend the majority of your time with (just as Jesus did with the 12 disciples). For example, Deion Sanders is a great friend of mine. When I say great, I mean great! A few years ago, when all the madness started happening, he was one of the first people to check on me. Unexpectedly, he jumped on a plane from wherever he was and flew to Atlanta. He walked into my office and said, "Hey man, I just wanted to make sure you're alright and to let you know I'm here if you need me." Then, just as quickly, he turned and jumped on the next flight out of town. Now, that's what I call a friend.

F.A.T. Friends is an acronym I created to summarize the key traits any friend should possess:

F.—Faithful

- My real friends—When situations happen, they never question me. For them, it was just important to let me know "I'm here."
- Faithful friends are protectors.

A.—Available

- A friend is available at all hours of the night.

T.—Teachable

- Real friendships can't develop if both individuals aren't willing to be vulnerable.

If I were to list some additional essential characteristics of a friend they would be:

- A true friend is always going to fight for you.

- A true friend believes in you.

- A true friend supports you no matter what is happening around you.

- A true friend is a protector—their natural instinct is to shield you from harm.

- A true friend prays for you and with you.

- A true friend is someone who is easy to talk to because you feel understood.

With the younger generation, they're always using the expression in their casual conversations, "You feel me?" or "You know what I'm sayin'?" What they're begging for is someone to talk to them, to be heard, and to be understood.

Darren Hardy's book *The Compound Effect* reinforces the importance of finding and surrounding yourself with people who can bring out the best in you. In his book, he outlines some key concepts on friendship and the people we associate with. More specifically, he says everyone is affected by three kinds of influences:

1) Input (what you feed your mind)
2) Associations (the people you spend time with)
3) Environment (your surroundings)[4]

These three influences, according to the author, will either bless you or curse you.

Taking this a step further, God said there is a difference between a kingdom relationship and a church relationship. Not knowing the difference between the two is where many people run into problems. Too many of us have church relationships instead of kingdom relationships.

While the principles of love and forgiveness are preached in the church, many of us do not embody these principles in our daily walk. We exhibit behavior that is contrary to what the Bible teaches. A real friend, for example, will embrace what they like in you as well as what they don't like. Thus, when we elevate ourselves to a kingdom mentality, we embrace the *treasure* and the *dirt* that sometimes covers it. When we're having Kingdom

---

4 Hardy, Darren. *The Compound Effect.* Vanguard Press; First Trade Paper Edition (October 2, 2012)

relationships, we don't get sidetracked by a person's shortcomings. As a real friend, we embrace the whole person and celebrate the good in them and try our best to dust them off when they fall down.

Having endured many trials and tribulations, the things I've learned about friends are clearly fixated in my mind. I was forced to study what it truly means to be a friend because I carried a lot of resentment, hurt and anger towards individuals whom I genuinely believed were my friends. These were people who I helped and gave so much to. Yet, they weren't there for me when I really needed them.

To my dismay, I saw how many people run from you in tough times. I was treated as a leper or someone with a contagious disease. No one wanted to be around me. Even those individuals whom I had helped greatly separated themselves from me. This is what made it hurt so deeply.

When something major happens in your life, you will be forced to reevaluate everything. One of the key areas of reconsideration can often be the sudden disconnect from people who have walked with you with for a long time. The feeling of abandonment can weigh you down and pull on your soul. I'm not talking about just regular acquaintances. I'm referring to the people who have walked with you, laughed with you, and cried with you. They have put in mileage with your life. Yet, it seems that when "it" happens, those relationships can come to an abrupt end. This was one of the most difficult aspects of my trial. For many of these relationships that ended, there was no conversation, explanation, or resolution. Even for me, after walking with the Lord for years, it was still hard to understand what God was doing in my life. How do I reconcile old relationships that were once meaningful, but just instantly dissolved? It's almost as if there were never a relationship.

Without a face to face meeting, these situations go unreconciled. For some of those cases, especially those without conversations, I've learned that it is important to take time to reconcile within yourself. You have to make a choice to let it go and move forward. Yes, there have been instances where I tried to reach back and rebuild relationships again. However, due to the breach of trust that both might feel, it was very difficult to reclaim.

There are times in our lives where we feel we have everything figured out. I have come to realize that we never have it all figured out. You will inevitably come to a major shift, a shuffling of the cards that will not make sense. You will be tested in every area. Those things and people that you swore by at one time, are now far from your grasp. Much of what you believe in disappears without warning. In these situations, it is important to manage your emotions. I cannot say how you will feel, but I can say that I felt a number of tangible emotions. I entertained the reality of rejection. Rejection and loneliness are emotional strongholds, especially when you're going through a devastating, life-changing situation. In the negative sense, what accompanies rejection is a strong heaviness that could lead to anger and depression. In the positive sense, this rejection puts you in a place of growth potential. You can be bitter, or you can be better. I call it "the moment when life interrogates you."

It is hard not to think, "How dare you?" to the people I lost. There were moments of grief, anxiety, and anger. I, unfortunately, fell into a place of not trusting anybody, making myself even more alone than I already was. I now realize that relationships are complicated. When you shut yourself down, it could be that people have abandoned you; or it could be that you pushed them away. In some instances, people didn't know how to reach out to me; because of that, they waited for me to reach out to them. Yet, because I didn't hear from them, I waited and became more disillusioned. As happens so often in our society, we all draw our conclusion. Before we knew it, so much time had elapsed that both parties had already come to conclusions that made it impossible to return. I am saddened that some of the separations were a result of "I don't know how to reach him, so I'll back up and wait."

My advice is when you see your friends are in a crisis situation, *never assume that people need to be left alone. Never assume that you need to back up until they call you. Never assume that you need to give them space. Let them tell you that they need space. As a matter of fact, force them to tell you to give them space. The time of crisis is the best moment to show that you care for them. Do not wait on the shore for your friends to yell, "Help!" when you know they're drowning.*

My advice to those who are in the midst of crisis is to never assume that your friends know how to deal with your trauma. Everyone is not going to have the perfect response. Give them the grace you desire. At least take the time to reach out to them and test the waters. If you're going to feel rejected, make sure it is real rather than imaginary. At that moment, you have to choose whether or not you want to let your friends go. Some people will only talk about what happened. You don't need a rehearsal of what happened in the past every day. You need people who speak to where you're going in your future, not where you have been in your past. They will help you make decisions and progress forward rather than remaining stuck.

There was a major lesson for me to learn. Through the process of introspection and self-analysis, I came to realize that I didn't do it to give... I did it to get. I needed to learn to give strictly from my heart without expecting anything in return. I needed to stop taking a tally of what I was giving to people. I also needed to learn, on a higher level, how to "let flesh get out of the way," so that I could fully heal and move on. I had to develop the ability to let go and know that some people are seasonal.

In the end, because I learned from it, it all worked out for the good. I'm more discerning of the people I let in my life and also more quickly able to distinguish between those who are placeholders and those who are kingdom relationships.

In learning what it means to be a true friend and what it means to genuinely give without expecting anything in return, I understand the purpose our friends and inner circle should have in our life. Friends, like family, offer us support and are intended to help us fulfill God's purposes. For those of us who are able to get just two or three kingdom relationships, we are truly blessed. It's like a man who finds a treasure in the field; he doesn't just have the blessing of owning the treasure, he buys and owns the field along with possessing the treasures found with it.

Chapter Three

WHAT I LEARNED ABOUT THE LAW

EDDIE L. LONG

There is man's law

and there is God's law.

Man's law is temporal.

God's law is infinite.

There are earthly judges

and there are heavenly judges.

Everyone, whether on earth or in heaven,

will be judged.

If not

for the power of Love,

no soul would be redeemed.

Love heals all wounds.

Love restores all souls.

Love rights any wrongs.

Love is the essence

of who we are

and what we are meant to be.

Love is what

we all are called to do.....

This is the greatest message

with which we are entrusted by God—

to Love unconditionally.

Love is the Greatest Law of God.

Bishop Eddie Long

Chapter Four

WHAT I LEARNED ABOUT FAMILY

The UNTOLD STORY
EDDIE L. LONG

Over the years, I've performed hundreds if not thousands of wedding ceremonies. During each wedding ceremony, I recite this affirming statement to the bride and groom:

"You will stand in prosperity and adversity."

Why do I feel compelled to share these specific words? Because I know that storms are coming. This is why building a strong family is necessary. In our greatest storms, our family anchor is our anchor.

Marriage and the vows of a husband and wife are more than just binding. They are the key building blocks for establishing strong family systems. But—as evidenced by a more than fifty-percent divorce rate in America—these bonds are often not strong enough to weather the inevitable storms. Many marriages do well in prosperity, but it's another story in adversity and turmoil.

When, in an hour, my life changed from being celebrated to being ridiculed, if it wasn't for my family, I wouldn't have survived. Faith in God was essential, but, the tangible, physical presence of my family was what I needed to anchor me. My wife, in particular, proved to be a woman of faith and unconditional love. She easily could have focused on herself and her own needs. Instead, she focused on my needs and how to be emotionally supportive.

The actions of my wife are representative of the extensive research that has been conducted on families. When families are intact, the benefits for adults and children are overwhelming. For fathers in particular, married fathers tend to have better psychological well-being. For children, research on the family indicates that:

> "The married home tends to provide a safer and healthier home environment. On average, children in intact families' fare better in school, exhibit fewer behavioral problems, and are more likely to form healthy romantic relationships as adults."[1]

Here, in stressing the importance of family, I want to be certain not to understate the significance of my wife's role in helping our entire family weather the storm. She made a major sacrifice in putting her emotional needs to the side and directing her energy towards keeping the

1 http://familyfacts.org/briefs/6/benefits-of-family-for-children-and-adults

entire family focused on moving forward. When you think about it, in a way, I'm my wife's pastor. Who does my wife go to when the current problem or issue she's coping with is the pastor? Where does she go to vent?

I could feel seeing me hurt pained her deeply. As a woman, I could also tell that she was protecting her own heart just to be strong for me and the family. I feared the long-term consequences of her carrying the pain of it all on a much deeper level than she would ever fully express. Yet, through it all, she somehow summoned the strength to weather the storm.

Let me be honest with you: our marriage did suffer during this ordeal. At one point, under the weight of the extreme stress and turmoil, my wife did leave for a while, and we contemplated divorce. What we thought would be 30 days turned into over a year of media harassment and, as a result, stress cracks developed in our relationship. The constant rumors and reports, at times, wore us down. This was not a result of arguments and anger, but it was a product of pain and pressure. Beyond the other elements of suffering, this was my greatest area of pain.

Our relationship did not consist of constant arguing and anger, but it doesn't always take that for a relationship to fail. I understood my wife's pain. She looked at me several times with tears in her eyes and pleaded, "Can we just leave and get away from it all?". She knew I couldn't evacuate the situation even though she was desperate for relief. This was our moment of reckoning. No matter how famous a person may be, no one is a superhero. We all endure private pain and public pressure. That's just life. Yet, where we take that pain determines our destination.

Thankfully, God gave us grace to persevere through our trial. We took the situation one day at a time and were ardently committed to reconciling with each other. We came out of this valley better and with a stronger union. Even in the midst of your darkest season there is life for you, if you refuse to give up.

Admirably, even my kids demonstrated a fortitude that I never imagined. They literally circled the wagons and became practical in how to approach the crisis as a family unit. Their heart was to make sure we got through it all in one piece and with a sound mind. All my kids became very resourceful in looking for ways to successfully navigate the crisis. They never questioned me. They were of the mindset that we just needed to keep moving forward and focus our attention on how to make it through the catastrophe.

Even my biological brothers stepped up to the plate. They were amazingly supportive and were not shaken by any of the events. My siblings and I have always been close, but the strength of our bond was proven on an entirely new level by the way they stood by me with whatever I needed. Truly, I know that I am blessed to have true brothers and the best family.

Because I was used to being able to exert a certain amount of control and power over my life circumstances, I was going through a period in which I felt a sense of helplessness. This, however, was just one of those situations where I had to take cover and wait out the storm. The most defenseless feeling was not being unable to shield my family from the chaos that surrounded me. When you love someone and view them as family, your first instinct is always to protect. To an even greater degree, as a father you instantly engage in protective measures. I tried to protect my family the best I could, but there was only so much I could do. It was a tremendously sobering experience.

The media pressure was so unbearable that I had to relocate my family to a new home to get away from it all. It was grueling. On top of this, I experienced the pain of witnessing what my daughter had to go through as a senior in high school. This was supposed to be her moment, a time of concluding her formative years and elevating, but instead, it was being dominated by my current life soap opera.

Seeing these difficulties firsthand, I knew I couldn't be selfish and focus on myself. Even though I was trying to be strong while refusing to throw in the towel, I had to rise above the urge to remain stuck in a state of self-pity and continue to be a faithful parent and husband to emotionally support my family. I had to embrace rather than run from the added challenge of ministering to each of my children in their own unique way. I had to give individual attention and respond to each of them accordingly.

This is one major lesson I learned about family: all children are different. One child may struggle greatly and

The **UNTOLD STORY**
EDDIE L. LONG

have a difficult time with the crisis. The other may handle it and function more adequately. You have to vigilantly assess their emotional and psychological state in order to accurately determine the best way to respond. My daughter, for example, just needed me to hold her. My second youngest son just needed to hear me say that I was happy on the phone. My middle son had his own challenges in dealing with it but did a pretty admirable job of adjusting given the circumstances.

Foremost, I had to be open to creating an environment for my children to talk. With the media frenzy and backlash, I needed to understand that I wasn't the only one being hit. They were being hit from many different angles as well. They have social lives and had to deal with public stares, glares and negative comments just like I did.

Even with all of the family support that was available to me, there were times that I questioned if it was worth it to keep living. My calendar went from being constantly full to completely empty. It was such a devastating blow that I literally thought about checking out. Life had put me in a valley of interrogation and I was desperately trying to find

55

a way out of the mess. I was so preoccupied with self and asking God "Why me?" that it felt like everything around me was slowly dying.

I was at my lowest point. What kept me going was feeding off the energy of my family. They kept me strong, and it was God's voice speaking to me that encouraged me to hold on and move forward.

I also reflected on how millions of our ancestors died on the voyage, in the bowels of the ships. We were stacked on top of one another like roaches, urinating on one another and suffering from dehydration. Only the strongest survived. This is the blood line I inherited.

God was reminding me that even in our darkest hours, there is always something to live for. That something to live for in my case is *family*. God's design is that we establish and build upon our roots. Strengthening our families is part of the calling on every individual's life.

Not everyone is as blessed as I am to have the family and support system. This is true of my blood relatives and of the other individuals whom we have adopted into our family. That shows just how powerful family support is; it doesn't necessarily have to come from the womb. Those whom we call family can be based on love and shared community.

As busy as I have been over the years, I owe all the credit to my wife for the strength and closeness of my family and it's because of all the sacrifices she has made through the years. Instead of placing our kids in private schools or having nannies, my wife stayed home most of the time. This provided the glue that keeps our family bonds strong. Little did I know that much later in life, I would face such trying times and that the difference maker would not just be the strength of my faith but also the strength of my family.

Chapter Five
WHAT I LEARNED ABOUT THE CHURCH

"God is a God of restoration.

What was lost

can only be regained

when God decides to restore it.

God has equipped the church

to be resilient.

God now wants to restore the church

from being a broken body

of individual kingdoms

to one unified Kingdom of God."

Bishop Eddie Long

"Thank You New Birth Church!!!"

I want to personally thank all members

past and present!!!

We built a great church at New Birth.

And, it wouldn't have been possible

without the individual contributions

of each and every member.

So, I say, "Thank You"

to those who are still there

and also to those who left.

I understand

and respect the fact that

we all have to work out

our own salvation.

I do not condemn. I do not judge.

If I were in their shoes,

I do not know

if I would not have done the same thing.

What I do know

is that God continues to perform miracles.

God continues to use New Birth as a tool

to carry his message of life,

love and deliverance.

Bishop Eddie Long

New Birth church is a blessed place. And for the last twenty years I have been blessed beyond measure to lead this ministry. In this time, we've done many great things within the greater Atlanta community and throughout the world. Most of the ways in which we have blessed others have been done without much fanfare, if any at all. We didn't do it to get recognition. We did these things—often spontaneously, at the spur of the moment—because we felt it was the right thing to do and because God put us in a position to be a blessing to others. However, I feel this is the perfect time to note some of the historic moments that have taken place at New Birth and highlight some ways in which we have given back to the community over the years. These are some of my proudest moments:

1. The four Presidents of the United States that spoke in the pulpit of New Birth Church were Jimmy Carter, Jr., George H. W. Bush, William J. Clinton, George W. Bush. Also, Senator Barack H. Obama, who later became our nation's first black President, was in attendance.

2. The honor of conducting the homecoming of Coretta Scott King

3. Holding Easter Sunday service in the Georgia Dome for several years

4. When Hosea Williams—a legendary civil rights leader from Atlanta—died, there was no money to bury him. The church paid for his burial without telling anyone.

5. After the passing of Hosea Williams, New Birth church made a $100,000 donation/

contribution to the Hosea Feed the Hungry and Homeless non-profit foundation which is widely known in Atlanta for providing hot meals, haircuts, clothing, and other services for the needy on Thanksgiving, Christmas, Martin Luther King, Jr. Day and Easter Sunday each year for a significant number of years.

6. When called upon by former Mayor Shirley Franklin and Ambassador Andrew Young in in their efforts to buy Martin Luther King, Jr's historical collection of papers (writings), we financially contributed to the "Backup Pledge" to purchase the invaluable papers and pay off the loan.

7. We have been a contributor to the Trumpet Awards for a number of years.

8. We have been the highest church donor in the South East for the American Red Cross over the last ten years.

9. We've purchased uniforms for various high schools in the greater Atlanta area.

10. We've built weight rooms for various athletic

programs throughout the city.

11. We've purchased cars for individuals and families in need.

12. The value of our ministry can also be felt around the world as we've opened a hospital in Kenya.

13. We've built a Business Trade School in Kenya along with a Convention Center where students can work in a trade.

So many great things have been accomplished through the ministry of New Birth and God is not done using us to be a blessing to others. God is restoring me, and God is restoring New Birth as we grow our ministry.

At its height, New Birth had a core membership of 25,000 and currently has 8,000 to 10,000 members. Thus, it is only human to at times feel a sense of disappointment in not seeing those seats as filled as they once were. Yet, what I do know, from having gained a greater sense of humility, is that those empty seats serve as a reminder of what "God" once did, not what Eddie Long did. It is also a reminder that God's measuring stick differs from man's. God starts with the heart. That's what God wants, our heart...all of it.

Today, I can say that God has more of my heart than ever before. And, the heart of the members of New Birth is strong as well. It is because of their love for God and belief in his promise, we were able to weather the storm.

Thousands of members left immediately in the aftermath of the allegations. Others left six months to a year later in response to peer pressure from co-workers or even from having to endure the discomfort of coming to church and being greeted by picket sign-waving protesters. For many, this just proved to be too much to bear.

On the flip side of this, there are many other members who felt it was more than worth it to hang in there and not give up. They believed that New Birth was still called to do great work in the Atlanta community and throughout the world. They believed in God's "promise" for New Birth.

The single most defining word that comes to mind for how New Birth is even still standing today and thriving is "resilience." The church displayed this in astonishing ways and stood firm on a new foundation.

Having served in the ministry for several decades, I've heard countless stories of pastors committing suicide or church doors closing when experiencing financial hardship and tough times with regards to leadership. However, that isn't the story of New Birth. New Birth has weathered the storm and is even stronger now than it was before. We, in fact, are having some of the best services we've had in the history of the church. Souls are still being saved, and we're continuously preparing disciples to go out into the world and spread the Gospel.

Resilience can be defined in many ways, but I think the definition below is the most fitting for what I have witnessed at New Birth:

> "The ability to roll with the punches. When stress, adversity or trauma strikes, you still experience anger, grief and pain, but you're able to keep functioning — both physically and psychologically.[1]

Without question, there still are deep wounds and scars

---

1 http://www.mayoclinic.org/tests-procedures/resilience-training/in-depth/resilience/art-20046311

from which we are recovering. Somehow—in the midst of all the turmoil and turbulence—we found a way to move forward reinvigorated by a clearer sense of purpose.

With that being said, if I could go back in time, I wouldn't change the backlash that I received. I now accept that sometimes you have to go through the storm, because the greatest growth comes out of conflict. This is how God's purposes are fulfilled. They are fulfilled through full restoration and true redemption.

While our human instinct is to avoid pain and conflict, it is often a prerequisite for shaping us into who God wants us to be. For example, Peter wanted to kill a man when they went to arrest Jesus. Yet, we now know that Christ dying on the cross was inevitable. It was his destiny.[2] It, however, is symbolic of the fact that "people will love you away from your destiny" because they don't want to see you hurt; out of love they will attempt to protect you and shield you without considering the higher purposes that are being fulfilled.

Many events in our lives are unavoidable because

2 Luke 22:49-53

God allows them to occur. Joseph was arrogant and that's what greatly angered his brothers. His arrogance made his brothers his enemy, but that started a course for his destiny. After being sold into slavery, Joseph spent years in jail. During this time, he was being prepared for something much greater than he could know. God was using Joseph's arrogance to humble him so he could fulfill His plan.[3]

Celebrity status can cause you to make choices that create scenarios for destruction. If I had made different decisions, I would not have found myself in the situation I was facing. God, however, used my limitations as a tool for bringing greater glory to His Name.

By going through such adversity, New Birth was given the opportunity to show the world what the church is about. We got the opportunity to show the world what God's church can look like. As we became the #1 Google Search in the world for a few days, we had the opportunity to show the world how God's people should deal with fellow brothers and sisters. We were able to demonstrate resilience, forgiveness, love, and a strong community. We

3 Genesis 37-50

took a hard hit, but we stayed strong and kept moving forward. We're a living testimony of how people can rise up, even in the midst of confusion and doubt.

All of this was done directly in the face of ridicule. Instead of being torn apart, we pulled together. The church didn't get distracted by the slings and arrows coming from the outside, instead the church held on to "God's Promise" for New Birth. We found strength in God's Word and in one another. The church, overall, functioned well and rose up in the power of love. A prayer line assembled every day inside and around the church that was filled with thousands of people who extended themselves with the passion of love and the power of faith.

And, to our surprise, hundreds of thousands of people from around the world also rose up in support of us. On more than one occasion, Prophet Samuel Abiara, an African Prophet came to Atlanta at his own expense. He would visit me and I would sit as his feet as he we would read scriptures that spoke to my soul and pray for me. He would then fly back to Nigeria only to surprise me a few months later with another unexpected visit with the goal of ministering to me and encouraging my faith.

This type of support kept me alive. The church at large had judged me. The media had judged me. The world had judged me. But, here it is—this man I had never met before—coming to speak into me in a way I never previously experienced. It was this type of support from the church that kept me standing.

One of the key things I have learned about the church is that there is always going to be trouble. When we think back to the founding of the early church, it started with Jesus and his twelve disciples. So, Jesus literally started with twelve members in his church. And, we all know— because it is chronicled time and time again—the conflicts and issues that existed among these disciples, are notably, within the church.

What this, then, tells us is that there are different roles that must be performed within the church so that it is fully prepared and equipped to address the issues that arise among its members. Jesus was not just a preacher and a healer. He was a teacher. He was a counselor. He was a big brother. He was a father-figure. He was a businessman.

The church must embody all the traits of Jesus. We must not only embody love and compassion. We must also embody the skills of restoration and reconciliation, which in itself, is a process. It takes time to put things back together after they have been broken, but, this is what God does. God restores that which has been broken.

What I now understand even better is that it is not the job of Eddie Long to be everything. I have to see the church as a collective whole made up of many parts. It is my job to identify the strengths and weaknesses of each of these individual parts and to strengthen them so that the entire church is as strong as possible.

We have to be open to combining the best of the old church with a new modern approach. Some of what we are doing to reach the community nowadays is obsolete and is outdated. We need a new model and a paradigm shift for reaching the current generation.

The best analogy I can give you is when I worked at Ford Motor Company. Part of my job function involved visiting different plants around the country, but I mainly focused on the southeast. For an interval of two weeks each year, twenty-four of the Ford/Lincoln/Mercury dealerships shut down their entire factories to retool for the new cars that would be in production. This was done at a huge expense, but it was vitally important.

This concept of retooling can easily be applied to the church. If business people know you have to retool and remodel a factory, then why wouldn't the church understand and apply this same principle as well? Because we don't view the Body of Christ, the church, as a fluid organization, the church never retools. So, we're continually addressing new models of people with old models of church; and, with limited success.

Much of my purpose lies in this area. God told me I am supposed to help retool and restructure the church, which includes watching young pastors grow and helping them stand. Thus, a big step in this direction is building a retreat center for pastors. Just as I painfully had to learn to see my role more as equipping the church to do the work of God, rather than feeling I have to try and do everything, this dilemma is being experienced by many other pastors around the world. It is important to help them understand God's perfect design for the church and how it is flexible enough to adjust to the changing times we find ourselves in.

It's also vital to help pastors learn to move out of their comfort zones and be willing to take risks as leaders. Ever since I first started out as a preacher, I had a radical mindset. I always took risks and felt we had to do things like build a gym to attract the community to our church. Everyone didn't agree, but I stood firm that the church couldn't do just the same old ordinary things if we were going to grow.

While the church needs to become more loving, the church also needs to become more strategic. I believe this can only occur if our perspective of the church dramatically shifts. This shift begins by recognizing God has already laid out a design for the church, and it doesn't consist of a bunch of individual kingdoms. God's design is one kingdom working together. This, I believe, is God's message to the church. We need to stop operating from an old "obsolete" church model, and we need to work together to build one kingdom of God.

Chapter Six

WHAT I LEARNED ABOUT GOD

"Before I formed you in the womb I knew you,

before you were born I set you apart;

I appointed you as a prophet to the nations."

Jeremiah 1:5

New International Version (NIV)

God has a promise for everyone's life. From the day we are born, this is our most fundamental life mission—to discover it and to fulfill it. It is helpful to remember that we are simply a spirit that is living inside of a body. Before God released us into time and set us on our life journey, God gave us a promise. God's Word says:

"Before I formed you in the womb I knew you, before you were born I set you apart;   I appointed you as a prophet to the nations."[1]

This is my message to you. *Live your life with the confidence that you were born with a promise.* Know and believe that even if your life is currently filled with darkness, God will bring the light. Even if you have been lost and abandoned, have faith that God will restore you.

You might feel like giving up and throwing in the towel——because you're weary, frustrated and don't understand why you're going through all the tribulations you're going through— but that's not what God wants for you. God wants you to see past your circumstances. God wants you to see the solution to your problem through spiritual eyes not through your eyes of the material world. Then, and only then, will you see that your "promise" is always bigger than your problem.

Every day, all around the world—and since the beginning of time—God uses adversity to build character, to make us stronger, and ultimately to glorify His Name. Even when we make mistakes, get off path, or waver in our faith, God will use our moments of weakness and our times of disobedience to humble us back to the path of fulfilling His "promise." The theme of the power of God's "promise" is seen over and over in the Bible. Even Jesus despised the shame that was going to come to Him through the cross. It was God's promise that gave Him the power to go through with it.

Once again, we find God's promise in the story of David conquering Goliath. David's confidence came not from his own power but from the promise of God.[2]

---

2 1 Samuel 17

These stories of God fulfilling His promise in people were a reminder to me during my toughest days and lowest moments that my life was not over because of social media or intentional attacks to discredit me. They were reminders that God will fulfill your promise as long as you stay with Him. Instead of hiding or crawling into a corner, what got me through was holding on to that promise.

Reflecting on when I first became a preacher, I initially ran from the calling. My father was a Baptist preacher, and that was honestly the last thing I wanted to do. So, I ran from it and suffered major consequences. I took a beating from God and eventually surrendered. I said to God "If you give me a wife, I'll be a preacher." God gave me a wife, but the marriage didn't last. I ended up divorced and broke. God's message to me was "Don't ever tell me what you need. Just do it." From then on, I just believed.

Prior to accepting my calling to preach, I majored in Marketing and Business and then worked for Ford and Honeywell. I didn't start preaching because I was broke. It's because God had another plan. Behind God's plan, there is always more than just the inspiration of the Holy Ghost. You still have to update yourself with skills to give the Holy Ghost something to work with. That's what God did with me. He took my business skills and used them within my ministry.

When I arrived at New Birth, I was surrounded by ministry minds. This was highly beneficial but at the same, in some areas, we had some strong disagreements. There were around 300 people in the church, and I had some very radical ideas about how to grow the church. My vision was big and my faith was high. In the end, the growth of New Birth surpassed anything I ever could have imagined.

What I learned from this was not to put your faith in man but to place your faith in God. God is the one who has the master plan for your life. Even if you've gone off course, God can put you back on course. God made me, and God has the power to break me. This was a very painful lesson and truth that I needed to be reminded of.

What I have learned about God and my understanding of how God works has deepened my understanding of the Scriptures. A very popular verse we like to quote, for example, is found in the book of John: *"The thief comes only to steal and kill and destroy. I came that they may have life and have it more abundantly."*[3]

My newfound understanding of this passage is that God, as a God of restoration, sometimes "allows" the thief to come in and do what he wants to do. He lets the thief come in so that God can then "restore us" and get the glory. God brings the dead back to life. He has mastered the process of death, burial and resurrection and uses it to his glory just as he did with the life of Jesus. People may have tried to judge me by what they think I did wrong in my life. God, however, judges me by what I have done right in my life. We, therefore, need to "remember what God remembers and forget what God forgets."

In your life you will experience "seasons" of crucifixion—basically, the process of death, burial and resurrection. Understand and accept this. Put your focus on never allowing yourself to stay buried in the death. Trust and believe that there always is "life after death." It ain't over until God says it's over. If I can get up, you can too.

It's never about the circumstances you're facing; that's not where you should focus your attention. It's

---

3 John 10:10

about the "promise." Hold on to your promise, and hold on to God's Word.

Because of what I've gone through, I'm more focused, and I know God better. This experience helped solidify my purpose. It put me in a position where I had to learn again to rely on God, and it removed many limits that I placed on him. I am now at a place in my life where I am totally reliant on who He is. This was only possible because I developed resilience and a much stronger faith.

God will restore us, but we have to be willing to do the work He restores us to. Because I continued to show up at the church even when people were calling for me to resign, my faith muscles became stronger. A lot of people give up on life not just because they lose hope, but they give up because they don't have clarity about the promise God has for their lives. You too need to continue to show up when you know the "promise" that God has given you.

I not only had to exercise greater faith, but I also had to deal with the inner man and take responsibility for many of the decisions I made that attracted the negative circumstances into my life. A big part of this was GOING TO

COUNSELING.

I needed to push through my problems and circumstances, and having someone to talk through stuff in a safe environment proved invaluable. I had been wounded emotionally and psychologically, and I needed to own it. I needed to put my pride aside and ask for help to get through the emotional trauma.

Too many times, we hear of men not going to the doctor or not talking about their emotional problems or physical ailments. They live in a state of denial to the point that they jeopardize their long-term well-being. My initial reservation or resistance to confiding in friends and family members was that I didn't want to be an additional burden to them. They were already dealing with enough and trying to do their best to cope with what I was going to. So, going to counseling offered a great alternative by taking a lot of added pressure off my closest relationships.

Honesty and self-reflection has made me a humbler person. It has allowed me to own many of my flaws. It was a necessary process that required me to shed the old in order to embrace the new. In order for me to move into the new dimension that God had prepared for me, I had to get rid of the past. If I were going to move into my new future, I had to be willing to fully let go.

I became so conditioned when traveling on a trip, my first instinct was to go to baggage claim and pick up my old baggage. However, it became apparent to me that it was time to get new luggage. It was time for me to surround myself with an entirely new group of friends and to get a whole new spiritual wardrobe.

As you grow, you have to be stripped and re-clothed. We have to be made vulnerable enough to know that God is in control of our life journey which includes knowing when to re-shape us and re-mold us into better people. Unfortunately, many of us try to short circuit or bypass the process. Some people want to wear diapers as adults and not endure the pain of the change. We opt to avoid pain instead of going through it.

When faced with a huge problem, it can be extremely difficult to see past it. When enduring trials and tribulations, we have to recondition our minds to know and believe that "the promise is always bigger than the problem." When we are confronted with a big problem, we have to have a mindset that there must be a much bigger promise on the other side than we're even imagining.

I found my way to the other side and was resurrected because I held on to His ultimate promise. Now, my greatest message to the church is, "We don't have much time." We have to take our hands off the wheel. We can't just preach restitution and recovery. We have to practice it. We have to believe in the story and the power of Lazarus.[4]

Lazarus died, was buried, and rose from the dead. We have to believe that drug addicts can be healed of substance abuse. We have to believe marriages that are headed for divorce can be mended and "rebirthed" into love and joy. We have to believe youth who are lost in the judicial system—where everyone has given up on them and counted them out—can find love, comfort and a sanctuary in the church.

Over the last few years, I've learned many lessons about myself, about family, about friends and about the church. Most importantly, *I've learned that God is a God of love and restoration.* Love and restoration is God's highest calling for us as individuals and for the church as a whole.

The UNTOLD STORY

The Story of Adversity, Pain, and Resilience

ALTAR CALL

EDDIE L. LONG

The challenges I have gone through in my life

were not just for me.

It was to birth life in others.

I don't know where you are in life,

but I want you to know,

"It ain't over!"

You still have a promise.

You still have a life purpose to fulfill.

Your reading this book is not by accident

but by divine appointment.

This is your divine appointment

and your divine turnaround.

And, I'm claiming that your death is over

and your burial is over.

Your resurrection has already occurred.

It has already begun when you picked up this book.

Bishop Eddie Long

Amos 3:3

CPSIA information can be obtained
at www.ICGtesting.com
Printed in the USA
LVOW04s0005110616
492136LV00002B/2/P